UNFILTERED *Diamonds*

FOR THE NEXT GENERATION
The Ivey/Low Connection

SUSIN W. PETERSON

Esquire Publications
13720 Old Saint Augustine Road #8-322
Jacksonville, FL 32258-7414
www.esquirepublications.com
Tel: 1-800-501-7640

"Unfiltered Diamonds for the Next Generation"

Edited By: Georgia Editing Service, LLC

Book and Cover Design By: Designs Unparallel, LLC
www.designsunparallel.com

Copyright © 2024 by Susin W. Peterson

This book is a work of nonfiction. All rights reserved. Printed in the United States of America. No part of this book may be used or reproduced in any manner without the publisher's written permission.

Library of Congress Control Number: 2024905036
ISBN: 979-8-9900739-2-0

UNFILTERED
Diamonds

FOR THE NEXT GENERATION
The Ivey/Low Connection

SUSIN W. PETERSON

INTRODUCTION

2 Chronicles 7:14 - My memoir is dedicated to my parents, the late great Ralph, and Pastor Maye Witherspoon. This is one of the mother's final messages that she left with my family. She foretold the future and shared that it would save our world if we abided by this rule.

"If my people who are called by my name will humble themselves, and pray and seek my face, and turn from their wicked ways; then will I hear from heaven, and I will forgive their sins, and heal their land."

My mother explained this contingency plan's conditions; she said it is all in plan writing if you look at verse 13 first. It is demonstrated that *"if I shut up heaven that there be no rain, or if I command the locusts to devour the land, or if I send pestilence among my people,"* there are signs that will be displayed. Still, if people follow God's instructions, this world can be saved. The signs are all here, along with earthquakes in diverse (many) places, and the seasons are beginning to clash.

Soon, we will not be able to tell the change of seasons; by the budding of the trees, the weather is becoming more and more unpredictable. I was told that these are some of the signs that we are living in the last days, are we? Because humans do not recognize the signs, creation is what our creator feels.

Thank you for the legacy that you left behind. I am still determining if I can follow in your footsteps, but I will attempt to live like you. Without them, I want to pay homage to a few other people near and dear to my heart. My life would have taken another path, Aunt Patronia Thompson. Aunt Judy Bright, the late great Carrol Ivey, her husband Uncle Arthur Ivey, who saved my life, and Aunt Dr. Judy Ivey, who cared for me as a grown person when no one else saw me in need.

Thank you, and I love everyone.

FAMILY HISTORY

FAMILY HISTORIAN

Dr. Horace Spencer Ivey is a husband, father, and grandfather. He is not only my uncle, but he is our family historian. Uncle Horace is my mother's eldest brother and grandson of Jonah Ivey.

He holds the title of clinician, has his Ph.D., and is a Professor at Upstate Medical Center. He was an associate professor in rehabilitation medicine who covered 21 counties and some locations in Canada.

He was on the American Medical Hospital Association Board and Chairman of the Division Board of Certified Social Workers Department. Horace was also an active member of the NAACP and was honored to do international work in Cuba because of their free healthcare system. Before families in Cuba were discharged from the hospital, a survey of families was requested. I understand this information would be used for statistics and data collection.

Horace earned his Ph.D. from Boston College School of Social Work. He was privileged to write policies, procedures, and standards for social work nationally and internationally.

The inspiration for my family history in this memoir is set in motion by this incredible Man of God.

Thank you, Uncle Horace, for contributing to our family, studying, and implementing social work.

Your work has not been in vain.

SOMETHING TO TALK ABOUT...

I want to give you something to talk about. My foundation and humble beginnings led to this present-day generation. The Zow/Ivey connection earned their freedom, land, and sense of pride with blood, sweat, tears, and, for some, even their lives. They all stood up for their beliefs, even while some were drunk. A certain amount of respect came from the name tied to their names that led to this legacy. The trickle-down effect that my family name has created helped build America. My family has doctors, attorneys, dealers, investigators, historical figures like Richard Allen, who helped establish AME Church; Brookins, who helped found Edward Waters College; actors who assisted with breaking racial barriers like Ossie Davis, preachers, heads of the police force, a mayor, city commissioners, principals, event planners, and nurses.

We must not let the dream of Dr. Martin Luther King, Jr., our forefathers, and other influencers die. It is my greatest desire to share the greatness that this family holds. I am asking that every adult share this information with each of their children, each one teaching one the significant influences that brought us to this present day and time.

Although our original religion is Hindu, we have been raised with the true and living God. Keep believing in the God of Abraham, Isaac, and Jacob. The God that brought the Israelites out of Egypt. The God that we serve of peace, not war, love, not hate.

Educate your children about our history and share who their family members are. May the God I just shared with you forever keep and protect you and your immediate families permanently. In 2000 A.D., Jesus Christ died on the cross for all our sins, so let's stop trying to take His place.

On November 23, 2021, as the pandemic ended, I had the opportunity to celebrate via phone with my uncle during his birthday dinner. His children were in attendance for his 90th birthday. My uncle still drives and loves to travel to visit with his children. He is constantly studying our history and gives updates on new things discovered. Some information my memoir shares is directly from him, and some has been passed down from generation to generation. My uncle is brilliant, with a doctorate in psychology, and my Aunt Judy, his wife, is the author of several books.

He recently flew to Florida from Upstate New York to assist me with putting the final touches on this memoir. Thank you, Uncle Horace. May God continue to bless you and keep you.

My family has made great strides and accomplished many positive goals. My family has actors, founders of religious sectors, medical doctors, and persons who have earned doctorates in psychology, teachers, nurses, pastors, investigators, social service counselors, police officers, financial advisors, contractors, homemakers, and entrepreneurs.

On September 6, 2023, I called Uncle Horace and my Aunt Judy to gather information and find out how he was doing, and with a cheerful voice, he shared that he was tremendously blessed. He thanked his grandmother, Amanda Brookins-Ivey, and spoke about how she prayed for everyone. He mentioned that she was the mother of her African Methodist Episcopalian Church.

 I had this conversation with my Uncle Horace Ivey, the family historian, about three years ago. We had many discussions over the years, but he mentioned a distant relative I still cannot confirm but want to say.

Our historian has a resource that took us back for hundreds of years. But it is not confirmed that Queen Nefertiti may be related to the Zow/Zoe part of my family. The thing is that this beautiful female Pharaoh is believed to be the other of King Tut. Her origins cannot be traced, but we know that she was the wife of King Akhenaten and, for some time, ruled Egypt.

Her stunning features symbolize ancient Egypt's beauty and, to this day, inspire cosmetics. She was probably born around 1360 B.C. to a military family.

    About 200 years ago, according to Uncle Horace, our family originated on a tropical paradise off the coast of Madagascar (Africa). In the middle of the Indian Ocean is a beautiful Island called Mauritius. This island has a spectacular underwater waterfall that can only be seen by airplane. The official religion is Hindu, and it remains the same today. This island has beautiful botanical gardens, luxury resorts, and amenities where you can swim with dolphins, go hiking, eat fresh seafood daily, and watch native dancers perform their native songs.

    We are the original natives of this island 9,793 miles from Deland, Florida, where we are currently. The Zow family was taken from Mauritius Island, sold into slavery, and then brought to the United States, only to be brought to Houston County, Georgia (near Macon). The family was split again, and some were sent to Virginia. The remainder was taken to Live Oak, Florida area, where enslaver and great, great grandfather Robert Ivey took my great, great grandmother, Sally (Mamie), to his plantation to work the fields. It is on this plantation that my great-grandfather Jonas Ivey was born in 1864 at the end of slavery and carried the family name of Ivey, which all his children have.

Great Grandmother Mamie Zow/Sister Vancy Zow-Lewis

My great, great grandpop had a sister with the married last name McIntosh; her husband was a doctor. My Aunt Susan Dawson said she taught them to read and write. In those days, she could have gotten into serious trouble because enslaved people were not allowed to read or write.

A large portion of the Ivey family was raised on the Suwannee River. I cannot confirm this, but it was shared that a person with the name of Ivey suggested naming the Suwannee River. My grandparents and the Zow side of my family rode into Volusia County, Florida, on horses. They were asked to change their name but refused. The family now resides in many parts of the United States, but it is here in Deland, Florida, that we stand at least one thousand strong.

Edgar & J.C. Ivey

HABAKKUK

Writing the vision and making it plain resonates with me as I read this Bible verse. The vision is for an appointed time, but at the end, it shall speak and not lie, though it tarry. Wait for it because the just shall live by faith. This is precisely the message that I am trying to relay to the world, and especially to my family and friends, about my life experiences.

The purpose of this memoir is to leave a legacy for the next generation of Zows/Iveys and a long list of other family members. The purpose is to connect the dots from Mauritius Island off the coast of Madagascar, Africa, which sits in the middle of the Indian Ocean, to Deland, Florida, over nine thousand miles from home.

Here, the main religion is Hinduism, where there is an underground waterfall. A place that is now rich and famous, where my family was taken from. It is now where luxury resorts reside. The way to enter this location, I have been told, is by way of Dubai. Dubai is another location on my bucket list since it is in the area.

A recent message from one of our government officials shared that certain parts of my Black History should not be shared. I will share all my history with family, friends, children, and grandchildren.

All history should be shared; we all have a story to tell, whether good, bad, or indifferent.

Everyone is someone special!

HISTORIC TIMELINE

To give an idea of when the timeline began, let's use the date that President Abraham Lincoln, the 16th President of the United States, signed the Emancipation Proclamation that ended slavery in 1863.

I. My great, great (paternal) grandfather, Robert Ivey, Sr., was born in 1845.

II. My great, great (maternal) grandmother was born Sally; some say Dolly (Mamie) Harvey-Zow was born in Virginia and sold to Robert Ivey, Sr.

III. My great-grandfather, Jonas Ivey, married Amanda Brookins in 1867.

IV. My (paternal) great-grandmother, Amanda Brookins, was born in 1829 and died in 1919. Her father's name was Robert Brookins.

V. My great grandparents, Jonas and Amanda Ivey, married and had many children; my grandfather was Arthur Ivey, Sr. He lived from 1909-1990.

VI. My (maternal) grandmother was Darleatha Zow, and Arthur Ivey had (10) ten children; she lived from 1913-1972.

VII. The father to Darletha Zow was Arthur Zow. He lived from 1880-1953, and her siblings were Jackie Bess-Zow and Hattie Alberry-Zow of Miami, Florida, and born to Arthur Zow was Sam Zow.

It is from these excellent unions that the great Ivey/Zow connection began and continues to this day in the small town of Deland, Florida. There are estimated to be a thousand or more relatives with many more names attached to these family names. There are too many to recall, and I apologize if your last name was missed. Still, suppose you are from the Ivey, Zow, Dawson, Murphy, Carter, Collier, Bright, Grayson, Cohen, Alexander, McIntosh, McClean, Williams, Davis, Witherspoon, Thompson, Keys, Jones, Jordan, Casminski, Rice, Wyche, Taylor, Bean, Thomas, Bess, Alberry clan. In that case, there is an extreme possibility that you may be related to me.

This book is about our family history, my personal experiences, and words of wisdom to pass on to the next generation. Please share this information with your kids, grandkids, and other relatives so that our history cycle is recovered and intact over time.

This is my written memoir.

Jonah Ivey-Patriarch of Ivey Clan

Grand Pop Arthur Ivey, Horace & Albert

Uncle Horace, Ruth & Betsy

CHRISTMAS IN OVERTOWN, MIAMI DURING THE 1970s

Who says living in Overtown, Miami, was not fun? In the mid-1970s, we would drive from Dania, Florida, to Overtown, Miami, where my two aunts (grandmothers' sisters) and their children lived. I love to visit with my aunts and cousins. Aunt Jackie lived in the first apartment on the second floor. We could look across the streets and see where Dr. Martin Luther King, Jr. preached one of his final sermons. My Aunt Hattie lived on the other end of the second floor. The tiny apartments were filled with joy, kids, and people from all walks of life.

Professional people, pastors, relatives, and friends down to the local drunks stood in line for a plate of food. My aunts fed everyone. There would be extra card tables with cakes, pies, and puddings, and other tables would hold greens, macaroni and cheese, string beans, rice gravy, turkey, fried chicken, etc. Another neighbor also treated me like her niece, who lived in the middle of the second floor.

We would go from one apartment to the next all day, eating, talking, playing music, and people-watching from upstairs. My Aunt Jackie took me to Miami's first Goombay Festival in Miami, Florida. After many years of living in Overtown, my Aunt Hattie's husband passed away. The two sisters purchased a lovely home on 131 Street, where the party slowed down but did not stop. They continued to have dinner parties during some holidays, and as soon as their old friends found out where they lived, food and fun were served.

Aunt Jackie Bess & My Mother Gladys Ivey-Witherspoon

4 MARQUEE CUT DIAMONDS

TYREE, BRIAN, GERARD, & LAMESHA...

During the late 1980s, four-diamond siblings came to live with me with one garbage bag of personal items and a raggedy stuffed teddy bear that was missing one eye. The stuffing was falling out of it. My diamonds are now in their late thirties and mid-forties. I did not give birth to these precious jewels, but they fit into my life like family. They all have different personalities. Tyree is my nurturing, protective child and my eldest child and peacemaker. He became my mother's fishing partner and road dog. They would pack their bags and travel to Tarpon Springs, Hollywood, and Fort Lauderdale, Florida, to attend church and visit old friends. Tyree was my child who loved to dress up.

Brian is my quiet diamond. He does not like being in the sun or outside for too long in the heat. When I was pregnant with my daughter Amanda, Brian liked being around me. He never talked much, although he was probably my most observant child.

Gerard is my youngest boy and family comedian. He liked to make and build things. Once, he brought a pumpkin home from school that his teacher had given him just before Thanksgiving. He asked me if I would make him a pumpkin pie, and I told him no because we don't like pumpkins. Gerard looked at me and walked away. I thought for a minute; this child may never have anyone to make a pie with him again, so I called him back into the room.

I had him wash his hands so we could make his pumpkin pie. Gerard was so happy you would have thought it was Christmas. After making the pies, he wanted to share them with his teacher and grandparents. He treated the pie as if it were a newborn child. This was when I realized that no one had ever offered to make a pie with him. Gerard had been living with his biological grandmother; then he came to live with me. He began having problems in school, and at the age of eight, he did not recognize his name in writing if he was shown, nor did he know all his alphabets.

As I read his history, I learned he had spent his previous year sitting isolated from his peers in a corner. I asked permission to have him clinically evaluated; this is when I realized he needed another academic placement. Within 72 hours, thanks to my friend who had Gerard evaluated, he was given the correct placement and, in small increments, was able to make progress.

Brian came home and shared that Gerard was at the park, cursing everyone out. I told Brian to get Gerard. About thirty minutes later, Gerard walked through the house, gently closing the door. I asked him what took him so long to come home, and he said he was talking to Jesus. I told him he was talking to the right one because he needed all the help, and I sent him to his room. Gerard explained that he knew he was wrong, but Jesus forgave him, so why couldn't I? I was no longer angry.

Lamesha is now 37 years old and only one of two girls that I ever lived with. As I am writing this paragraph, Lamesha is calling me. She is sweet and needs attention. At last count, I have shared my life with eighteen children. All children need love and guidance. That is my motto.

LIFE EXTENDED 26 YEARS

During the 1980s, my mother had an injury to her foot that became infected because of her diabetes. For many months, she went to the doctor, but he said there was nothing else he could do to help her heal. With the assistance of my father's diligent efforts, he would keep her wounds clean and sanitized, but her injury was not getting healed. My mother became increasingly ill with vomiting and a very high fever; she was developing sepsis fast. My ex-boyfriend introduced me to a wonderful herbalist, RN Nurse, and woman of God named Mother Mary Fields. This lady, a stranger to us then, invited my mother to come to Orlando, Florida, to live with her until my mother became healthy. She knew with the progression of her wounds that time was of the essence.

On the drive to live with Mother Mary, my mother held a bucket in her lap for the duration of the ride of three hundred miles to vomit. She had become very weak. When we arrived with both of her arms around our necks, we carried her inside Mother Mary Fields' home.

Drinking water would not stay on my mother's stomach during this time. The incredible thing was that the woman taking care of my mother was bedridden and unable to walk due to a condition of the spine. She had an assistant who lived with her named Sister West. She took care of both my mother and Sister Mary.

Mother Fields immediately changed my mother's diet. She took her off sugar, white bread, no sodas, no junk food. If she had a sugar craving, she would be given graham crackers. She would have her assistant to mix and match certain herbs and teas. Her herbal cures would come from a very old book by Jethro Kloss called "Back to Eden." Mother Field's phone would ring from places like the Virgin Islands, Europe, and other foreign countries all night.

Although Mother Fields had her issues, she constantly prayed for others. I never saw her sleep. I would watch as my mother's wounds were cared for by my father with then slices of beef and betadine, and surgical solution until the next day while creating a wrap. Every so many hours, this cycle would be repeated. They took care of my mother like she was an infant. Thank God for the efforts of Mother Fields, my father, and my sister, West. My mother was able to live until 2009. She lived with us for 26 years longer than the doctors said that she would.

My great-grandfather, as a young married man, developed a taste for alcohol. He would get so drunk, walk into a bar, and demand a drink of liquor. Sometimes, he would attempt to carry my mother and uncle down through town with one child on each shoulder. The residents would shout, "JONAS! Put the children down before they get hurt". He would shout,

"These are my %@#?* grandchildren, and you can't tell me what to do!"

My great-grandfather was a tall, slender, handsome, biracial man with curly hair. Sometimes, he would get so drunk that he would fall off his horse. The horse would come to the house's front door without my great-grandpop because he had gotten too drunk to remain upright and would fall. My great-grandmother, Amanda, would send my grandfather and his brothers into the dark fields to retrieve and bring him home. I once overheard my grandfather say he hated going out after dark looking for him.

LIFE EXPERIENCE

The year 1992 was one of the most challenging years of my life. I did not know what direction I was going in as I navigated a very messy divorce. After my husband left home for work, I quickly got on the phone with the matriarch of the family, my mother. When she answered the phone, I quickly told her I could not take it anymore and was leaving. Mothers have their way of seeing things long before anyone else. "You should have been gone. I told you not to place all your eggs in one basket. Have you been saving and putting back your money?" My mother wanted to see Amanda and me before we left, so I told her to meet me at the drugstore, where I had to get Amanda's seizure medication. My daughter, Amanda, was born prematurely. Three days after she was born, she had a massive stroke with many complications.

I had no idea where we were going. I left home with a large purse filled with as much information as I could find, including a week's worth of underclothes in my baby's zip-up blanket, baby formula, water, essentials, pictures, my daughter's shot records, and a few other items of importance in the trunk of my car. I only had $80 to my name and purchased gas for the car I had bought during the summer. "Where are you going, Susin?" my mother asked. "Wherever the Lord leads," I replied. I knew I needed enough time to get hundreds of miles away before my husband realized I was gone forever. I gave my mother specific instructions not to return to her home because her house would be the first place he would look and terrorize. I had a feeling that as dark approached, he would not be nice to anyone in his path. I instructed my mother to live with her church friends in Orlando, Florida, and wait until my father could join her. She was living in South Florida at the time.

While in the drugstore parking lot, my mother handed me a bottle of green Gatorade and a small empty cooler; that was all she had, but her love was enough. She said a prayer with Amanda and me, and I will never forget her words, "Susin, stay with God."

I drove as fast as I could toward the Georgia line with no specific destination. I did not know if I would ever see my family again. I just knew one thing was that I could not go back. I drove until I reached Savannah, Georgia, and met with my mother's friend, a Pastor. When she first saw me, she did a double take because she did not recognize me, then yelled, "SUSIN!!" and told her members, this is Pastor Witherspoon's daughter. She immediately knew I was in trouble and took me into the Pastor's study to counsel me. I explained to her that I had to leave my husband to stay safe, and then I explained that I had a very ill child. She went into prayer mode. After she prayed the prayer of faith, she prophetically said, "You are safe here; he will not come here."

As soon as she finished talking with me, I recognized a pastor in the ministry. I shared my story, and she welcomed me to stay in her home. During my first night stay, I called my mother in Orlando to tell her that Amanda and I were safe in Savannah.

THE MATURITY OF PEACE

The peace that passes all understanding is what you feel when you have relinquished your power to be in control. When you must let go of the ideals that once had such powerful meaning. When your intended plans change, it leaves you scratching your head and feeling empty, wondering what to do next. With prayer and maybe patience. God can give you a plan as a way of escape and positive change.

It will allow you to remain sane and continue your daily routines without ever mentioning what you are going through to a soul. During my senior years (lately), I have cultivated being quiet. I have learned that if the other person cannot help you solve the problem, it is best not to share it.

Many people can inadvertently become dream killers; this is when negativity and gossip can creep in, forfeiting all hope of mature peace. Looking back over my life, I see very few things that I regret, although one is an honest regret. I always wanted to participate in the Armed Forces. I tried getting into the Army when I was about 38 years old. I also tried getting into law enforcement with Border Patrol but did not do well on the test. In 1992, I tried another form of law enforcement but did not understand the sequence of tests required to pass, although I then lived with a deputy. Then, at 43, I thought I would try to join the Army again. I spoke with a recruiter. After three questions, the recruiter said, "Ma'am under no circumstances will we enlist you in any branch of the armed forces." On that note, I never had the tenacity ever to try again. The messages were a sign that it was time to give up the idea of joining. It was only then that I had peace about this career move.

    Although I greatly desired to be trained to fight for our Country, it would not happen in this lifetime.

JACKSONVILLE CREW – EARTH STAR DIAMONDS OF SOUTH AFRICA

One morning, my boss, Ella, called me into her office and asked me to close the door. My first thoughts were that I must be in trouble or have done something wrong. She asked me to have a seat and told me about a basketball game she attended over the weekend at Stetson. She continued that the people there were cheering on the team and that there was an older lady who came from the bleachers and began cheering with the cheerleaders, kicking up her legs and walking up and down the basketball court, telling the players how to play and hot to shoot the ball.

My boss said that the lady had the entire audience captivated. It was all eyes on her and the people that came with her. Ella said she started inquiring about these people, wanting to know their origins. She learned that they were my relatives. She stated that she felt the game went down in history, not because of the game, but because of my relatives who entertained the entire crowd. I told her my family always liked having fun, and she assured me everyone had fun.

SIXTEEN-HOUR ORDEAL

Okay, so I fought with the orthopedic doctors for as long as I could, but Amanda has begun to have severe respiratory problems. Her back had become severely curved from scoliosis. The doctors wanted to place titanium steel rods into her back, and it was going to be a very long, drawn-out ordeal. I hated the thought of Amanda going through one more surgery, the last of many brain surgeries, and now, to keep her breathing, the doctors were suggesting doing a nine-hour back surgery. On the day of this surgery, my mother, father, aunt Judy, and mother West (mother's prayer warrior and good friend).

We all prayed, and with each passing hour, I had more anxiety than I ever had in my life. By the fifth hour, I was about to lose my mind. Every time the phone rang, I would jump up and run over to the phone, but it would not be for me for a total of sixteen hours later. It was awful watching my daughter trying to recover from this very long surgery. I appreciate all the support that family, friends, and clergy gave me and Amanda during this time, but I wish that it would not have been my child who experienced so much suffering. One of the things that scared me was that I did not receive a phone call like all the other patient families did. A team of doctors came out to speak with me, and while I was in the hallway, down another hallway, I saw my daughter's eyes tapped down like a dead person and rushed to the ICU to recover.

By then, I was crazy because I had not seen her for sixteen hours. The doctors shared with me that she had to be given many pints of blood and had lost 96 percent of her blood. Hindsight is 20/20, but this is one of the surgeries that, if I could turn back the hands of time, I would not allow her to go through again. I stood in the hallway next to the very large picture window. I witnessed life flights, one after the other, delivering organs to different parts of the country to people who required them. How I know about this mission, is that I had the opportunity on the same day to meet one of just a few persons in the world that were born with multiple organs, this was mentioned in my first book. It took Amanda about two months and a few follow-up visits before I began to see her play and smile again. This ordeal was torturous, and it may have been unnecessary.

THE MEADOW

Around the year 2005, I had a fantastic dream. My daughter Amanda had passed away about years before the dream. I dreamed that my daughter came to me and tapped me on the shoulders. She held me by my hand, and as we walked across the bedroom floor, my roof became the open sky. My daughter pointed up, so we went higher; I could feel the wind on my face. It felt warm and comfortable like being wrapped in a blanket. As we descended, a little boy stood with his back turned to me; he never turned around for the duration of the dream.

When our feet hit the ground, we landed on a beautiful meadow on a fast-moving river. The water was cool to my feet. My daughter pointed, and massive-sized goldfish came up to me, allowing me to pet them; in the trees, there were panda bears and koala bears, and deer would come to the edge of the river, allowing me to touch and pet them. I tried looking into the face of the little boy, who appeared to be about five or six years old, but each time I would get close, he would not allow me to see his face. Amanda escorted me around the meadow, but after some time, she said Mother, it is time to return. I did not want to return home but knew that contact with me would be limited because we now live in two different worlds.

Once again, she pointed upward, and we began gliding through the clouds. The warm breeze was on

Amanda's face. She had grown into a beautiful young adult. When I awoke, I felt refreshed, not tired, and holding onto the side of my bed as if I had just landed. I am not one hundred percent sure of the meaning of my dream, but I know that when I can see and remember colors in my dreams, then they are prophetic; when I do not remember if my dream is in color or not, then it is usually just a dream. I have had a few other dreams since Amanda passed, but not like this beautiful dream. Amanda, I love and miss you, honey.

SAVING LIVES (IN THE NAME OF JESUS, IT WAS ALREADY DONE!)

Around 2005, I attended a service at Bishop Al Jones' church. I sat listening to different prophesies being shared. Bishop Al came to me and said, Susin, stand up. I stood in humble submission with my hands lifted over my head. He said, Sue, I hate to tell you this, then I changed his mind and said no, I don't because what I am about to tell you will save your life. He said something that sounded very confusing to me. It was that he failed to protect me. I began scratching my head because I had no idea what he was talking about. As I looked at Bishop, he asked, "Did they see me tell me he had a girlfriend because he left me vulnerable? Then, he asked me a very important question every woman should ask before getting involved with any man. Bishop asked me, Susin, did you ask him if he was involved with anyone? I said yes, this was my second question; my first question was, are you married? He said no, I am not involved with anyone, and I am not married. I trusted that he told me the truth because I met him at church. We were still on church property when these questions were asked. I am very private and would not make it a habit of talking about private matters, but you could hear a pin drop during this very public moment. All eyes were on me.

Bishop said, Susin, I see you going to Orlando to visit him. This woman is blocking you in his driveway. He said I could see your boyfriend trying to defend you, but he would not be unsuccessful. Bishop said this woman hates you (this person I have never seen before) because he brags about you when he is in her presence. Bishop then gave me a word of warning by saying not to go back to Orlando. Do you hear me? I said yes, sir. He said I see as she blocks you in the driveway and she approaches you, she begins to stab you repeatedly. I hear them calling your relatives from the coroner's office to identify your body. Bishop said to come up here and let's pray the prayer of faith and protection. He concluded in the name of Jesus. It is already done! The remainder of the church service was complete silence.

A few months before this prophecy, I tried talking to my then-boyfriend about getting married because we had been dating for two years. He looked at me sternly and said I will not marry you now or ever. I said OKAY but did not argue; I cried when he was not around. At the time, I did not understand why he was acting the way he was acting, but after the prophecy, it all became crystal clear.

After this time, I did not hear from him for about two months. When he came to visit me, I saw a knot on his neck about the size of a dime; the next time, it was the size of a quarter because I only saw him if he traveled to come to see me. I would only see him occasionally if he traveled to see me, so I was not traveling to Orlando. He was a chain smoker as well, and he smoked more than he ate.

About four months after this, he called from Winter Park, Florida Hospital to say he did not have long to be here. He asked me if I would visit with him. I told him that I was sorry that he was ill but would need to call back before visiting him. I called Bishop and explained that he was in the hospital. I then asked if it was okay to visit him there. He said yes, Susin, he is sick now. Visit him, but do not linger. Make it short, then get your butt in your car and leave. I thanked Bishop and let him know that I would need to take my father riding with me, and God knows that I do not want anything to happen to him. He lived for about 24 months before I got the call that he had passed away.

CELEBRITY
CHATLINE

A celebrity embraced me, and since 1999, I have been reading the books of a particular celebrity and author. There is one book of hers that I have read eight times. Every time that I lose someone close to me, I will re-read this book, and each time that I read it, I will see information that I did not see or pay attention to the time before this author went to heaven, over forty years ago, she shared her visitation with her audience and returned with information that will blow the American people away, that has suffered a loss of a loved one.

It was about this time in my life that my daughter's doctors began trying to prepare me for her demise; I refused to accept this information and, for the most part, ignored the inevitable, but this author gave me great hope. I was able to handle the passing of my daughter because this author gave me a picturesque place where my daughter would reside until I arrived to be at her side.

She described in detail her encounter of not being here on earth. She shared the love that she felt from God, she spoke about the spiritual guides that she was introduced to, and they escorted her to certain parts of heaven. She told the audience how God wanted us to love each other and how we would be given assignments and new clothing once we arrived. She also briefly forewarned us of things on earth that would happen if we did not amend our ways and begin to care for each other.

When she returned to earth, she had a unique garment made that emulated something she saw or was a part of her heritage. I was shocked because it was almost exactly like a garment that my mother spoke about and made after she had a dream about some library she had gone to. My mother said that an angel opened the book and showed her name; she said that it was called the Book of Life.

This author shared that the colors were very bright and could not compare with our dull colors on Earth. I was intrigued by this author and vowed to meet her someday. I tried to contact her by e-mail several times, but her information would always return undelivered. By chance, I went onto her website just to get an update. Off and on for a few weeks, I would get information about her podcast.

Just by chance, a thought came to me to reply one morning. The following day, she returned a response to my reply. I told her that she had been a great help to me when my daughter was so ill and thanked her for sharing her story. She gave me such great peace by saying Susin, you will see her again one day. Boy, I smiled all day long and told a few close friends.

A few days later, she invited me to her podcast (zoom); there I was, sitting in front of this very kind celebrity; she was kind, accommodating, and chatted with the audience. I was so dumb that I just stared at her, smiling, and staring. Guess what? Almost fifty years later, this person's story is consistent; she shares the same story, and I love her approach to life.

CATFISH STEW OR LOVE?

Late one night, while listening to a radio prayer line, my phone rang, and surprisingly, it was the person I was listening to on the prayer line. His very first words were, "I finally found my wife." I almost hung up, thinking the person on the other line had made a mistake call. Just as I was about to hang up the phone, he spoke with me superficially about the desires of his heart. It was a general conversation and just getting to know each other. Gradually, I would get a phone call when I thought I would not hear from him anymore. Since October 16, 2016, I have been in touch with my fiancé. This was the title he gave me. After a few weeks of talking, I was beginning to look forward to a future with this man of God.

Sometime during 2015, I started watching him on YouTube. I watched secretly because this minister is much younger than me. I did not want anyone to know how infatuated I was with this young man. My friend looked over my shoulder at them, praying for people on YouTube. I quickly left this site so he would not respond to how he prayed for people. Once, I received a message that his ministry would be nearby in 2015. I knew that I had to find him. I got a friend to ride with me to the service, but I had to leave early because the nurse caring for my father's shift was about to end. I thought that 2015 would be my only chance to see him.

I know that you must be wondering what happened to this relationship. We did not grow as close as I would have liked for it to grow, but we stayed in communication. I heard him hear from me every few days, and his words were always encouraging. Although I thought I would not see him again on January 7, 2017, I got to see him again publicly. His message was, "Sight is Connected to the Call." He shared how God will always place things that he wants you to reach for outside of your comfort zone. He said that you must see whatever you need from God before you receive it, Genesis 13:14.

On November 11, 2017, my fiancé said the Lord spoke with him about me. He then asked me if I would be willing to move to Texas and if I would marry him at the end of 2018. Of course, I said yes. He explained that temptations would be tremendous but felt he could overcome any distractions with God's help. I explained that I had nothing to offer but would be willing to accept a new life with him. He traveled the world with one of his mentors to do ministry. During this time, he spent lots of time in the United Kingdom. The time in the UK differs from ours, but we would talk for hours and plan our future together. It is difficult to explain, but the proposal given never came to fruition. We both agreed that our bond was very strong.

The minister is highly prophetic; even as I write this portion of my book about him, he is calling. Sometimes, I would think about a subject without mentioning it to anyone; he would tell me what I was thinking. With a very gentle approach, he shared with me about the final hours, what I would see before my father passed, and how to handle the situation. When we were together, he would tell me if he liked what I was wearing and said he could see the corner at work that I prayed in each morning.

One might ask me to get over it and move on. One might ask me if I am angry; I am not. You do not understand that our bond is like no other one I have ever known. Although a marriage did not take place, we remain distant platonic friends. To protect the person's family name and his reputation, I cannot reveal his identity, but you can take a guess: Catfish Stew or Love?

GREEKTOWN AND SUMMER DAYS

Once, she went to a funeral at a Greek Orthodox Church in Tarpon Springs, Florida. My parents would allow me to visit sometime during the summer months. I would walk over to St. Michael's Church, where many miracles had occurred. There is an icon of the Virgin Mary that will cry just before disaster strikes. There was a funeral, and Susan and Clara stepped in line with the deceased's family and sat with them. They all walked up to the casket and kissed the deceased. It was about this time that Aunt Susan decided to faint because she did not want to kiss the deceased. The family stopped attending to the deceased family members to attend to my aunt. On the walk home, Aunt Clara asked my Aunt Susan, *sister, whose funeral we had just attended.* Clara said, *I thought you knew.* They laughed it off.

My Aunt Susan attempted to teach me how to make homemade buttermilk biscuits. She removed all the ingredients and demonstrated. I stood by the stove impatiently waiting for my biscuits and syrup and could not eat one biscuit; they were so hard that the chickens hanging around the back door for food would not touch them. She always wore an apron with pockets. She took her shot glass out of her pocket and laughed at my business with a drink of whatever she had in her cabinet.

I remember my Uncle Jewel from South Carolina and my other Uncle Fred living in the same house. Uncle Jewel worked the railroads but could not drive. My other uncle would drive everyone to their destinations. It seemed like he was always driving my Aunt Susan whenever she wanted to go, but only if she would cook for him. When they went on vacation, Uncle Jewel and Uncle Fred would drive. It would be the funniest thing to see all three in the front bucket seats of a Chevy Impala. At seventy, Aunt Susan came to my graduation in Hollywood, Florida. The next day, we all went swimming in the Atlantic Ocean. Aunt Susan could outswim me. I asked her how she learned to swim like that. She said that on her way home from school, they would hang their clothes on a tree branch; sometimes, the loggers would float logs on the Suwanee River, and one by one, they would push each other into the river with the hope that they could reach the log. Susan said, I know it sounds stupid because we did not think about drowning; we just jumped in the water hoping we could reach a log. Once she left for home, I wrote her a letter thanking her for attending my graduation. Some months later, she opened a savings account of about $1500 for me for college.

When my aunt visited me, we would always have a great time. All my cousins from my generation loved to hang out with her because it did not seem to matter what the subject was. She knew how to have fun and enjoy life. She lived to be 96 years old, and to this day, I cannot think of one soul who knows how to love, laugh, and enjoy life as much as she did.

    Once Aunt Susan had a visitor to show up at her house, she came to the front screened door and asked may I help you? The stranger said, Ms…is your name Mrs. Williams? She said no; he asked if she was born in ??? She said yes, and he said I am sure I am in the right place. Aunt Susan said that she became afraid and wondered what this man wanted. He said I think that you were married to Mr. ??? Williams in ??? she completely fell out of her chair laughing because she forgot that when she was 13, she married a man, got on the train, and dumped him a few stops away. She shared that back in the day, if you had someone to take care of you and got married, you did not have to work in the fields. She said that she was a child and did not know anything about marriage and did not want to get married. She just wanted to be free. My Aunt Susan could have written a bestseller on relationships because she lived her life just how she wanted.

ZUMBA FOR SENIORS

Zumba classes had been canceled due to Covid-19. I loved to dance and would get in trouble as a child because my mother was a preacher, and dancing was prohibited. She would catch me snapping, popping my fingers, and moving to some song and saying, " You better get your mind on Jesus." I have been exercising for many years, but this class is my go-to outlet and workout. My Zumba instructor recently resumed classes. Trust me, although I continued to exercise, when I returned to Zumba, some of the moves I could make pre-Covid were ten times more difficult as a Senior. Having my instructor (Certified Trainer) come to our rescue has been a blessing.

When I first started attending, I thought that I was in great shape and could keep up without a problem; let me tell you something: after my first few classes, I walked around like I needed extra oxygen and CPR. Zumba, for me, is an excellent social outlet. We meet faithfully as if we were going to church. My instructor is lovely; her students literally follow her from location to location, and classes are packed to capacity. She plays lots of Spanish and West Indies music, and she does not allow you to get bored because just when you feel that you have learned all the moves, she will come up with something new, and you will swear that you are at a club. One night, I casually spoke with this lady who said it was her night to attend another class, but she told another member that she was going to Zumba.

I look forward to attending on Saturdays.

MISSED AUDITION

As I watched a superhero movie, I was reminded of the days I had a talent agent. I received an important phone call from my agent sometime in 2015, asking me if I was ready to have a chance to audition with a very popular actor, along with other actors. Information was shared that a portion of the movie would be filmed in Orlando, Florida, and the last half would be filmed in China. This would be the movie's last cast showing for this character.

The terms of the audition were verbally agreed on; I was told that I would be given a series of three phone calls, and with each call, it would mean that I was closer to being chosen to audition for the part. After the second call, I became excited because I knew that the third call would mean that I would be given instructions on the type of character, the location to meet, and the date of the opening premiere. The third call for this movie never came, although I did receive a few more opportunities to audition in a few movies.

ANYONE WANT A CORONA?
NO THANK YOU!!!!

During our crisis, I decided to take on a challenge I had been putting off for some time. Although I am working, things are slower than usual, and after many months of being unable to do anything personal, the time has finally arrived when I can work on my second memoir. I can work on the layout, preference, chapters, and conclusion. As we all know, this is a very serious time, and it is forcing all of us to slow down and prioritize, and if you are like me, live with less material things. The world has come to a time where rules no longer apply, and the nature of man is filled with deception and hate. Technology has advantages, but a lazy person can sit at a computer and steal everything you have worked hard for. The virus is taking the lives of many, closing schools, financial institutions, and even churches. Traveling is next to impossible. While taking the chance to travel, you may be asked to remain in quarantine, or you may return home in a casket. The list of things can go on and on when just ninety days ago, we could do anything we wanted to do if our money could pay for it.

A wise old mother tried to prepare me and my family for such a time as this. My mother was a Prophetess and had the uncanny ability to see the future and find scripture with the solutions to each problem. One of her favorite scriptures was:

2 Chronicles 7:14 "If my people, which are called by my name, shall humble themselves, and pray, and seek my face, and turn from their wicked ways; then will I hear from heaven, and will forgive their sin, and will heal their land."

She would often say that this is the solution to our problems. My mother would speak in parables and Bible scriptures all day long. To this day, I am so thankful for the foundation that she laid for me and my family. She is undoubtedly missed.

DAYTONA 500 WE LOST A GREAT RACE CAR DRIVER AND ALMOST LOST AMANDA

I will never forget this day. Amanda had been very sick for days. I had repeatedly taken her to the local hospital, and they kept discharging her, saying that she was fine, but her fever would not come down. She had stopped eating, she could not keep foods or drinks down, and she was increasingly becoming more lethargic; I knew that something was very wrong; if the hospital was saying that she was okay, why was I not able to keep her temperature regular? At this point, I am not sure what to do. I am just a layperson. By force, I am learning medical terms and what usually happens in most common and uncommon emergencies. This time, I am exhausted and at my wit's end. On the fourth day, I knew that my child could not handle much more, so I called her specialty hospital in Orlando, Florida, and left a message for her Neurosurgeon on the after-hours line, within minutes they returned my call with an urgent reply for me to bring her into the hospital immediately. I will never forget this was on a Sunday afternoon.

On the same day, we had lost a famous race car driver at the Daytona 500, and the 1-4 interstate was bumper-to-bumper traffic. Amanda's hair was soaking wet from the very high temperature. I wrapped my child up and tried to keep her comfortable; in the heavy traffic, she kept looking at me, but because she was not verbal, I did not understand the message she was trying to relay.

As we approached the St. Johns River, we got on the top of the bridge; my daughter took one look at me, took one very deep breath, and somehow came out of her seat belt and fell forward onto the floor of my truck. I managed to turn her over enough to look at her face, and she was purple. Her lips were blue, and I knew that she could not breathe. I was unsure what to do, and I could not think of what to do next. I was now on a bridge stuck in bumper-to-bumper traffic, I could not go to the left or the right, and if I blew my horn, I would make everyone furious because they would not understand the message that I was in trouble.

I screamed, "OH God!!! You have got to help me." I kept saying to myself that if I could just get to the bottom of the bridge, there would be a small hospital around the river. We were stuck on the bridge for about 45 minutes; I cried, screamed for God to help, and prayed. After 45 minutes, I got off the bridge and to the hospital, where they stabilized Amanda. They called her hospital in Orlando, where they sent their ambulance to retrieve Amanda. Once she arrived at the hospital, she was taken straight to the hospital, where she spent nearly one month trying to recover from a very bad shunt infection. This was one of my very scary moments; each time I speak about it, I see it and relive it. It makes me feel like I needed lots of prayer and a martini; I know the two do not go together, but that day, it felt like it.

PURPOSE

There are many ways to find your purpose, but let's look at the life of Jesus Christ. His life is the greatest example of purpose, although it is certainly on a different level. The example of this spiritual being having a human experience proliferated the entire world with the simple message of love, how to love, how to give love, and how to exemplify it. There are examples of Jesus Christ on every continent, state, and city. There are examples of the cross everywhere as you look at stories about what the cross means. Some private colleges and Universities will require classes about the life of Christ before you can graduate from their programs.

The purpose is always centered around your passion and the problems that you are meant to solve. You might ask how I know for sure what my passions are. Passion is when you are dog-tired of participating in whatever you are trying to do. Still, somehow, you find the time and strength to return to that activity designed to help someone else or solve a problem for a group of people. Working on your passion can sometimes rejuvenate you when it saps all the energy out of someone else who does not have the same passion as you. The job you are designed to solve may not allow you to make much money, but it is not entirely about money. No one else will be able to perform the job assigned to you just like you because whenever you are in the right area of your life, provision (money) will be provided for you, or your gift will make room for you.

VERBAL MEDICATIONS & NATURAL REMEDIES

I have been on a personal mission since 1999. My quest has been to study the biographies of persons who died and been resuscitated. I have been studying how to live life with purpose. The most outstanding example of this is the life and legacy of Jesus Christ. Through different experiences / I am learning how solace, peace, and fulfillment can be obtained and maintained. In one case study, a person who had a four-hour (NDE) or Near-Death Experience returned with the knowledge of how to prevent illness, although some illnesses will come as a gift to learn from the experience. I have been taught that giving too much of yourself can completely deplete you. When love is not returned, it perpetuates illness and creates resentment.

Essential things to learn and to teach your children are to love yourself, be positive, and be yourself because people generally respect you more when you respect yourself. Stop worrying about what others think of you. Just be yourself. If you have lost loved ones who passed away, they still hear us, and they love us unconditionally. I learned that every person has their own individual experience, some will be good, and for others, it may not be good. As relatives and loved ones are about to cross another realm, two possible worlds may be experienced. Still, the most important thing that I want you to remember and look for is that the dying person will make statements like" Eva came by to visit today," and Eva has been dead for fifty years. Or ask questions in the present tense, like has Ola gotten home from work yet? And Ola has been dead for twenty years. Deceased loved ones will start to visit to prepare them for their journey home.

I became most interested in this subject when I learned that my daughter would not have much time with me. I needed to know that she would be all right and her experience would be beautiful. L learned that in heaven, the architecture they have, beautiful colors, flowers, and gardens that are so spectacular that it does not compare to earth, and that there is no death once you arrive, and that knowledge is obtained instantly. During the devastating time of COVID-19, I have been on a personal quest to find natural remedies while we are here to survive and stay healthy. There are two nutrient-dense natural herbs that I recommend everyone to take if you are not allergic to shellfish.

Take it daily and look up the benefits of Organic Moringa and Sea Moss. Moringa is great for about 300 conditions, and they both will build the body's Immune system. I wish that I had known of these beautiful herbs years ago, to give to my parents and my child. I feel with certainty that these herbs could have extended their lives.

GOD'S TIMING

It is 10/19/2021; I have been reminiscing about the many deaths that have occurred due to COVID-19, the Delta Virus, and the many world disasters that took place in a short period of about 24 months.

These events changed the world. I thought about this for almost twenty consecutive years now living in crisis mode, taking care of immediate family members, and making life or death decisions for a family that could not do it for themselves. I feel most fortunate to have remained healthy enough to come to my family's aid. I learned many life-supporting skills and have been asked by a registered nurse if I were a nurse because of the nursing skills I learned over time. My heart bleeds for our world in its current state and morns for creation. My theory is that we live in the last days, even if it is the beginning of the end.

The Bible says that when we see earthquakes in (divers) many places, wars, and constant rebellion, we live in the last days. The increased storms and volcanic activity are all signs; just pick up your Bible and read it. A student told me that the Bible means **B**asic **I**nstructions **B**efore **L**eaving **E**arth. This is precisely what the Bible is; no other book on this planet is like it. The scary part is that included in my theory is that there will be many of the same conditions. 2 Chronicles 7:14 gives us a solution to our continuous decline in Earth's progress. The physical signs are in the 13th verse. It breaks my heart to hear about families that are unable to say goodbye to their loved ones, visiting them behind a glass wall or brass bars.

Children in our country have been orphaned due to this virus that does not have any respect for persons young, old, rich, and poor. Today, you are here; tomorrow, you are gone. We humans must change our ways and teach our children by living positive lives and being positive role models for them. The signs are apparent.

FORECLOSURE!!!
WHO ME?

Some years ago, I lived in a four-bedroom older home that I purchased in 1994. I loved this old home; it had three living rooms and, eventually, three bathrooms. For the duration of my stay in this home I remained single and never refinanced this home; during my final days there, I had severe things to think about because the roof needed repairs and the plumbing was not working as it should. My mortgage payments were falling behind, and I needed to find a way to quickly become current with payments, so I reached out to my family, and although they had their financial issues, they came to my rescue to help me make my mortgage current. Thanks family. I heard a voice telling me to walk around the house's perimeter and just look, so I did.

A tree branch was growing out of the sewer line attached to my home, and parts of my roof had begun to decay. I said a prayer, then went inside. When I entered the doors, I heard the words sell it. I said sell it, where will I go? I am a baby boomer, so I think you should hang on to what you have; the younger generation has a different mindset and will sell and leave in a heartbeat. I began my quest to try and find a realtor but dreaded the steps needed to sell my home. Then I had a thought that I would get some of the strong saints to pray about this matter. I did not trust everyone but confided in a relative who sent up a powerful prayer. She said one thing to me: It will be so easy until you do not believe it.

One day, I was listening to the radio, and a commercial came on with the name of the firm/ realtor that sells homes with a new format that is quick and easy. The website was shared. It asked me to upload pictures of my home. The next day, an appointment was made with their inspector to come and inspect my home. final submission of contracts and a ninety-day period to move was set; just that quickly, I was moving. I said all this to say that faith is the substance of things hoped for and the evidence of things not seen. I could not see the results, but he will do just that when you allow God to order your footsteps. Sometimes, he will only allow you to see as far as your rearview mirror allows you to see, and sometimes, your visibility will be zero; until you get closer, just stay in your lane and wait your turn.

WEARY IN WELL DOING

My prayer to you, my people, is never to get weary in well-doing. When you pray, try not ever to get tired. That old saying that God will not put more on you than you can bear is true. Looking back over my life and the times I played the caretaker role. My observation is that as each precious life that I cared for came to an end, my prayers became self-centered, especially as my body became tired.

When you get tired, please be careful how you pray because our heavenly father and his angels hear our prayers. God tends to continue to allow us to fight with vigor until our prayers weaken and begin to change. When we say the devil is a liar, he cannot have my child!! He will usually give us more time with that person unless his will for our lives is more significant than our desires, and the burden will become too overwhelming. When your prayers start changing to, "Oh God!! LET YOUR WILL BE DONE."

Watch out! God is coming to your rescue, and you can start counting the days; God is on the way to give you recuperative rest and peace, although it almost always hurts, especially when you start praying oh God, I am so tired, let you will be done.

As I grew weary while trying to do what was right with each personal loss, my prayers went from strong and vigorous to slowly saying, God, I do not know if I can do this anymore; I am so tired; please help me to hold out!

I recently said those exact words just about every day, and within 48 hours of my declaration, the Coronavirus hit and changed the entire world. I know it was not just because of me, but I used this as a parable to share how quickly God can and will intervene.

The most vivid time and memory was a time when my prayers began to change the last time that doctors wanted to do another major surgery on my daughter. At this point, I felt it was fruitless and had become about money. Amanda had stopped bouncing back, and her quality of life had greatly diminished. I was spending more time at the hospital and less time at home. Amanda's school had changed to a school for children who were medically fragile when she was well enough to attend. I got on my knees and prayed to God with this request, only that God's will be done and nothing else.

From the time that these words were spoken until she passed away about ten months later, I relinquished my will and allowed God to take my daughter to a place of peace and rest. Always let every prayer be sincere and respectful, and try not to get weary while doing the right thing. God will come to your rescue.

AURORA BUTTERFLIES OF PEACE DIAMONDS

I want to pay homage to those great Generals (Aurora Butterflies of Peach) in my life. Please take the time to look up these diamonds; they are natural diamonds that can be researched, and each one mentioned is stunning and of very high value. The diamonds mentioned are great supporters and have kept me close to them and lifted me in prayer.

My Late Mother, Pastor Mae Gladys-Witherspoon & My Late Father, Ralph Witherspoon

My late mother, Pastor Mae Gladys-Witherspoon, my late father, Ralph Witherspoon, Pastor Reba Smith, and Pastor Anita Collins of Dania and Fort Lauderdale, Florida. Pastors Burt Lancaster McBryde and First Lady Marie McBryde. My current Pastors are Apostle/and Pastor John and Sheila Hickman at the Mountain of Faith International Ministries.

Mother Ann Dawson was a prayer warrior who fasted and prayed continuously, asking God to keep our family together. Pastor Connie Robinson of the Open Doors to Christ Church, where my mother founded this church, is currently in Dania, Florida. Pastor Robinson picked up the torch and has supported me throughout my adult life.

In Loving Memory Of Mother Ann Dawson

During my losses and time of need, she would drive from Fort Lauderdale to Deland all in one day just to say hello, preach a funeral, or whatever needed to be done.

Thank you, Pastor, for being a part of my life. Dr. Kimberly Ford is a true friend, a fantastic artist who grew up with me. I can always count on her to give encouraging words and to check on me during the holidays. Bishop Al Jones can prophetically see in the dark and has been a part of my life for about 12 years. Keep shining bright, my diamonds; you are needed in this world for God's Kingdom, and my diamonds crossed over to the other side.

Thank you for holding the torch so we can see clearly over here.

THE CALL OF THE OWL

Some years later, I talked with my cousin, and she said, "Susin, there is something about the story of the Owls." It feels like they send us a warning message to our families that are about to cross over to the other side. She told me about her daughter, who was in her final days of life. She said that her daughter was in Hospice (an end-of-life facility), and while she was driving down the road, an owl flew out of a tree and landed on the hood of her truck; he refused to move. She found someone to take the owl off her car and then continued her route home; as soon as she got home, the hospice Center called to share the news that her daughter had just passed. Both my cousin's daughter and my biological daughter are in the arms of Jesus. An observation was made during the final days of my daughter's life. My parents called for me to pick my daughter up because she was just too ill to continue to sit upright in her wheelchair; they encouraged me to pick her up so that she could lie down and rest. My heart told me that she would not be back to visit with her grandparents and that she was living her final days.

As I brought her out of their home, there was a huge white barn owl in an oak tree, watching me bring my daughter out of their home as I placed her in the truck and rolled her wheelchair to the back. This is when I observed a large sliver barn owl in another tree watching me leave with my daughter. After we arrived home, I called her primary doctor; she called the hospice program of Volusia/Flagler County the same day. Amanda only lived for sixteen days after this call to hospice was Made, but I feel that she was at peace.

    When she gently raised her eyebrows and took her last breath, I felt that she had peace. I have never had that kind of encounter with owls again until April 2020. During April, for the entire month, I could hear owls outside of my bedroom window, multiple owls near my Crepe Myrtle tree. We all know what happened next. COVID-19 reared its head, and it has continued to take thousands of lives daily. It has changed our lives forever, and unemployment is high. I understand that every time a person dies, an entire library goes with that person. So set positive goals, help who you can, and try to share the knowledge as you learn.

CODE BLUE

Once, I was about to end my stay with visiting my daughter at the hospital. I was bathing her and had planned to go straight to work several counties away when I heard the nurses and doctors rushing around. Then I heard Code Blue!! All the doors to the other patient rooms automatically closed, but in the room where my daughter was close to the nurse's station because she was in critical care and had to be monitored closely, there was only a curtain. I could hear the crash cart rush past my daughter's room next door.

The nurse peeped into Amanda's room and said I am sorry, but you will need to leave I quickly asked, is there anything I can do? She asked can you speak Spanish? I said very little. She said go to the lobby and see if you can find this child's mother, calling her first name only; she does not speak English. Only say a prayer with her and tell her that we will visit with her. I went into the lobby because it was before six am, and few people were there. Still, when I called her name and then placed my hands in a position to pray, I said, let's pray, she quickly fell to her knees in the lobby, and I got beside her. We prayed, me in English because my Spanish is very poor. She gave me her undivided attention as we prayed; only God understood what we were saying. I gave her my name and held her hand. After praying, I knew I had to get onto I-4 before the traffic got too heavy, and then I left for work.

When I returned, my mind was on this precious little Spanish boy who had just moved here from another country. Because of confidentiality, I was not supposed to ask questions. My daughter was in ICU, and just about that time, she was being discharged to step down (lesser care). I finally saw the nurse who asked me to pray for this child and his mother about two weeks later. I said I knew that no one should be asking about what happens to other patients. How is the child doing? She looked around, then pulled me into the hallway; shaking her head, the nurse said he did not make it. He and his mother had just moved from Honduras, and the mother is a migrant worker; she does not have anything. I was almost sorry that I asked because my heart dropped; the nurse said thanks for praying with his mother; you were probably the only person there for her. I shared that it was no problem; this is what I do. I said that I was happy to assist.

ONE OF THE GENERALS HAS GONE HOME

One of the generals went home to be with the Lord. On March 19, 2023, after attending church, I received a disturbing phone call. One of my aunts called to share that my youngest aunt had just passed. Right where I was in the McDonald's parking lot, I lost my mind crying, and although another month has passed, I still cannot believe it. I was just a few blocks away from the hospital where they had taken her, so we jumped in the car and went to see her where the family had already arrived. Her eldest son and daughter-in-law were at her side already. I politely crawled into the bed with her. Her beautiful hair had turned platinum silver, and she greatly favored my mother in her most recent years.

Although she could not move around as freely as she used to. In my eyes, she was still young at 71 years old. She still went shopping and to church and visited family and friends. I never heard her complain. Since we were only eleven years apart, I just did not expect her to leave us so soon, but I guess the saying " you never know, tomorrow is not promised to us." She was there when I was born. She was there when I got married, she was there when my daughter was born, and with all the many surgeries that my daughter endured, she was there for most of them. One surgery was scheduled for eight hours but turned into 16 hours. I was so distraught until I sat by the surgery operating room door, waiting for them to come out with her. My aunt grabbed me and brought me back to my senses.

She knew what I was thinking and said, "Susin! Wait until they get Amanda stable." I returned to the waiting area. She was there when I had to sign the hospice contract for Amanda, and 16 days later, she was the first person through my doors to comfort me after Amanda had been taken to the funeral home. She was there for my divorce, and after my parent's health began to decline, for meals, and bath time, she was there. She was forever cleaning my parent's house and her house. When my mother passed away, her husband went and got her from work, and she was there.

Once Amanda stopped breathing in my mother's arms, she stopped by to visit, and my mother was walking around in the front yard, holding Amanda and praying. My aunt grabbed Amanda from my mother and did CPR until the ambulance came. When my father passed, I called her and said, "Auntie." she asked is it time? I said yes, and within 15 minutes, my aunt was there. For every significant event in my life, my aunt Cynthia, Judy, and Elizabeth Ivey-Bright were there for me. I just wish that I had more time with her. Do what you can for each other while you can. Auntie - "St. Matthew 25 Vs. 23 says well done, good faithful servant; thou hast been faithful over a few things, I will make you ruler over many." Rest in peace. Your work on earth has not been in vain. I love you.

AMAZING GRACE

It is God's Amazing Grace that allowed us to be here today. It was God's Amazing Grace! I do not understand what allowed me to be the only survivor of six siblings. God proved to me that his grace was sufficient even after I had a brother born sixteen years after me. He did not survive as well. It is God's Grace that allowed me to continue to keep my family and me healthy and safe. Along with God's grace, mercy, and favor. The favor of God is not fair but is needed to help our lives come into alignment with God's word and our true purpose.

The Bible gives many examples of God's grace, mercy, and favor. If you do not believe me, study the history of King Solomon and King David. What God has for you is for you because no one else can do what God has planned for you quite like anyone else. Even God's grace, purpose, and mercy for twins are similar but not the same. Covid-19 is, in a sense, a tragedy, but it will bring new faces, goals, and strengths to the forefront that otherwise would not have been noticed.

Let's face it: the entire world has changed overnight, historically more 'than since the days of Noah. It appears the Lord has decided to purge the world. The bottom line is that there is nothing new under the sun. History is repeating itself.

THE BLACK DANIEL BOONE MY TRILOGY DIAMOND (CAT EYE DIAMOND WITH NINE LIVES)

About 40 years ago, I met the African American version of Daniel Boone. He drove a raggedy motorcycle and a truck with holes in the floorboard so large that you could see the ground while driving. Tracey loved living in the woods, hunting deer, rattlesnakes, and women. Today, he said, "I am about to go fishing." There is something about this gentle giant that can soothe any person's fears, and at the same time, he can make you laugh. He is a gentleman, but at the same time, he has a way of telling you off if you get his timing wrong. If I wanted to find him, he would probably be somewhere on a horse, hunting in the woods, or camping. He also liked raising pit bulls; he was a natural Alpha. This man only worked for someone else once when he felt like it, but he was never broken and always had money. It appears money looked for him. Tracey would sometimes disappear for a few days, off on one of his adventures, but when he returned, I could always find him.

This is not a city boy; as a matter of fact, for many years, the only time that he would come to the city was to visit a relative or to come to his favorite Chinese restaurant. He knows how to have fun and how to treat a lady. He does not see color; this boy loves any flavor; if they are pretty, every woman falls in love with him, not just because of what he can do for them, but how he treats them. He has this ability to make all women feel like they are the only female on the planet.

Once, I went to a barbeque at his house. There were fifteen females there, all rolling their eyes at each other. After observing the atmosphere for about thirty minutes and feeling the resentment that you could cut with a knife. I decided to get out of Dodge. There was another time that I casually called and asked him, "Where have you been?" He said that he just wanted to get away. My imagination rode off into the sunset like Medusa's hair, but I decided not to question him. There was another time when he called me and asked, "What are you doing?" I said nothing, he said get dressed, we are going out. I forgot the name of the Country Western bar, but it was my first time going to a Western bar to dance. Tracey knew everyone in the bar.

This was my first experience with group line dancing. Most people think this was African American tradition, but I feel it started with the Country's Western culture, and I had a blast. On another occasion, Tracey asked me to come to the backwoods in Deleon Springs. When I arrived, there was a small group of his Caucasian friends swimming in a pond. Tracey asked me why I didn't wear my bathing suit. We got on this rubber dingy with a cord attached to a plank in the middle of the pond. After a while, I heard him say, "Uh, watch your leg; there is a gator." I was shaking like a leaf. This man has never been afraid of anything or anybody.

One night, after a long day of hunting in the woods, he asked me to come to his house. When I arrived, he was still outside sitting in his truck. He said, get in, he apologized for being a little dirty, but he had been in the woods all day. I am sitting in the truck, looking at the ground through the floorboards, and he says, I got something to show you. I immediately became afraid because I knew that he was wild; I knew that something was in this truck that used to be alive. He exited the truck and went to the back, right where my hand was. He pulled back the cover that lay across the truck; there was a sixteen-foot rattlesnake minus his head. I screamed!!!! Tracey got into a terrible accident. When I saw his parents in public, they asked me to visit.

For a long time, I was scared because I heard that an industrial-sized backhoe had fallen onto him and crushed his pelvis and other bones. About six months into his hospital stay, I finally decided to visit. He looked at me disappointedly and said, "Why haven't you come to visit me? did not have a good answer. He has had many surgeries and an open-heart surgery, but God is still in the plan.

Although sometimes he is in a great deal of pain, He is still mobile. He has five children and decided to move to another state. Yes, he lives in the woods in Tennessee with the Yetis, his favorite place to hang out on a four-wheeler, but when he comes to Florida, sometimes he will contact me. I think that we will always be friends.

LIFE STRATEGIES

As a senior, I am so sorry that it has taken me so many years to figure out how to stop surviving and enjoy the life God has granted me. It is my opinion that one of the best strategies for my life is to pray and ask God to follow in my footsteps. Do not wait for another person to make you happy; you will always be disappointed. The truth is that happiness comes from within. Set positive goals for yourself. Make sure that any extra work you take on fits like a glove with other life goals so you will not suffer burnout. If you are a parent, find respite care annually so you can do your best when it is time to return to work. You can do your best problem-solving by getting recuperative rest to assist with learning how to problem-solve at your best.

Keep a journal of things that work and make your life easier. Ladies, take time to take care of yourself and exercise when possible. Create a schedule that only belongs to you for an hour or two at least three or four times a week. For those of you who may need a little push with being creative, take a walk, attend Zumba classes, or buy cheap weights. At the same time, you watch T.V. and try to start each day by reading God's word; spiritual health is very important; most people do not realize that your spiritual health can be stunted, just like your physical health when it is neglected. Be a giver to the elderly single parents who may be struggling to feed their kids, and do not forget to include giving back to your place of worship.

At least once a year, plan a vacation that does not include your current environment, become more cultured, and learn about your history. Get a massage and take your vitamins to keep your immune strong. Keep the journey that God has given you here on earth as fun and eventful as possible because we do not have a long to be here. Life is a fleeting moment.

MY BLOOD RED
HOPE DIAMOND

I need to share my Blood Red Hope Diamond with you. It is my birthstone color and one of the most stunning diamonds I have ever seen. This jewel's name is Susan Dawson, the most prized aunt I have ever spent time with, my shero and confidant, although she lived in a different era. I emulated and vowed to live life to the fullest through her life because she taught me how. She also had a sister that she was close to, named Clara, but the party did not get started until Susan arrived.

These ladies were my grandfather's sisters. All the young people would invite them to their parties, and the young single ladies would often ask my Aunt Susan to babysit for them. I heard one girl ask my Aunt Susan; *how did you get this child to sleep after I left?* She waited until the girl left, then told me *she put a little beer in the baby bottle*. I said, *Aunt Sue, you can't do that! What if the baby had an allergic reaction to the beer?* She said, *Listen, honey, beer has been around for a long time; I bet you can't count the time on one hand when a child had too much.*

In Loving Memory Of Amanda Brianne Peterson & Elizabeth Cynthia Ivey Bright

Gone But Not Forgotten...

*In Loving Memory Of Elizabeth Cynthia Ivey-Bright,
Age Progressed & Regressed Photo*

*In Loving Memory Of Elizabeth Cynthia Ivey-Bright,
Age Progressed & Regressed Photo*

In Loving Memory Of Amanda Peterson,
Age Progressed & Regressed Photo

*In Loving Memory Of Amanda Peterson,
Age Progressed & Regressed Photo*